Winning Ways

for Early Childhood Professionals

Partnering with Families

Gigi Schweikert

Name: ____________________

Date: ____________________

Redleaf Press®
www.redleafpress.org
800-423-8309

Also in the Winning Ways series by Gigi Schweikert

Being a Professional
Becoming a Team Player
Being a Supervisor
Understanding Infants
Understanding Toddlers and Twos
Understanding Preschoolers
Supporting Positive Behavior
Responding to Behavior
Guiding Challenging Behavior

Published by Redleaf Press
10 Yorkton Court
St. Paul, MN 55117
www.redleafpress.org

First edition 2012
Cover design by Jim Handrigan
Cover photograph © diego cervo / Veer
Interior design by Erin Kirk New
Printed in the United States of America

Library of Congress Cataloging-in-Publication Data
Schweikert, Gigi, 1962–
Winning ways for early childhood professionals : partnering with families / Gigi Schweikert.
p. cm.
ISBN 978-1-60554-002-3 (alk. paper)
1. Early childhood education—Parent participation. 2. Early childhood educators—Professional relationships. I. Title.
LB1139.35.P37S4 2012
372.21—dc23
2011026613

Printed on acid-free paper

U20-10

Contents

From the Desk of Gigi Schweikert

This is me presenting.

Dear Winning Ways Reader (and Family Partner),

As an early childhood professional, I once hid in a closet to avoid a difficult parent—certainly not one of the shining moments during my long career working with young children. This Winning Ways book on partnering with families is not full of ideas on how to avoid parents or hide from them, but how to work well with families and come together, even when we disagree.

I know that you, like me, would do anything to help a child succeed. We guide children socially, emotionally, physically, and cognitively. The interesting thing is that the best way we can help children learn and grow over the long term is to work closely with their families.

When I was first teaching, I often thought, "As soon as I can get these parents out of the room, I can start teaching their children something." I just didn't realize that if I could influence and help a family, I could influence and help a child for a lifetime. Now I know that partnering with families is good for the parents, the child, and me.

There are still some families that make me want to head for the closet, but now I better understand that, despite the differences or personality clashes I might have with parents, we still have the same goal in mind: how can we help this child?

After you've read this Winning Ways book, send me your ideas on how to work with families and your own closet stories at www.gigischweikert.com.

Children deserve our winning ways,

Introduction

Do You Partner with Families?

You may be thinking, "Partnering with families, don't you mean partnering with parents?" I mean both. *Parents* typically refers to biological or adoptive adults who are legally responsible for a child. A guardian or foster parent may also be legally responsible for a child. But children may also have grandparents, neighbors, babysitters, or even adult siblings who play an important role in guiding and caring for the child. Those people who invest time in the lives of a child are also that child's family. It's great when young children have many people who love and care for them. So our responsibility as early childhood professionals is to know and work with all the people who take the children to the program, pick them up, attend program events, or spend time with them. For example, you may meet the parents of a child when he enrolls but see the neighbor every day because she drops off the child and picks him up. You need to know the parents and the neighbor—that's the family you are partnering with. Make sense?

For those adults who are not legally responsible for the child, make sure you have completed, written forms that give consent for them to drop off and pick up the child, spend time in the school, and learn information about the child and the program. Without written permission, you may never give out any information about the child or the program or release the child to the adult, even if the child knows the person and wants to go with them.

What Makes a Family Partnership?

Most early childhood professionals think they partner with families, since many define a partnership as teachers working with parents who follow the program rules, listen to center advice, and recognize the efforts and hard work of the staff. But a partnership is not a relationship in which one party tells the other party what to do and they do it. A partnership is a mutually respectful relationship in which parties take accountability for their responsibilities and work together to define and change the organization, based on a common goal. Sound complicated? Kind of, but let's define what partnering with families really means in early childhood education. It means intentionally working to establish individual relationships with each family and incorporating their family goals, values, and priorities into the program's culture. Partnering with a family is not you taking over the family but enhancing and supplementing what they are already providing for their child. You get to know the child and his family, and you use your experience and education to help that family and child receive the best care and education possible. You support the family.

Using This Book

This book is for anyone who works with young children and wants to make a difference in their lives, one that goes beyond the time the children are directly in your care. The book is comprised of seven sections to help you initiate that real parent partnership:

1. Know the Name of Each Parent
2. Welcome Each Parent
3. Develop an Individual Relationship with Each Parent
4. Care for the Parent to Help the Child
5. Keep Each Parent Informed
6. Create a Culture in Which Parents Can Share Ideas
7. Never Give Up on Helping a Parent

Children Come with Families

Ever play teacher when you were a child? Did you line up all your stuffed animals and dolls, even your younger brother, and play school for hours? Many early childhood professionals admit to playing teacher as the main focus of their imaginary play when they were young. And now here we are, early childhood professionals, doing the real thing with real kids. Yet when I look back on those fond memories of playing school, I never remember having stuffed animals that represented the parents. In fact, when I was an undergraduate about a hundred years ago, I don't even remember courses about working with the parents.

As an early childhood educator of young ones, however, I quickly found out that working with parents is as much a part of the job as working with kids, only the kids are cuter. Although I didn't bargain on the parents being a part of my role as an early childhood teacher, I did realize that every child has parents and someone has to bring them to school, especially since they can't drive and some of them can't even walk.

Caring for Parents Too

As a new teacher, I quickly accepted parents as the ones who were required to bring in the extra set of clothes, bake cupcakes for school parties, and turn in field trip permission slips on time. I liked the parents who brought in extra cupcakes for me to eat, gave me money or gift cards for holidays or for no reason at all, and followed all the rules. The parents who asked lots of questions, went crazy over lost pacifiers, and constantly hounded me about more academics were not my favorites. I thought parents were supposed to listen to me and do what I said, since I was the teacher.

I was wrong. After many years of experience, I still become annoyed by some parents, even though I'm no longer in the classroom. I also understand parents a bit more, having been a parent myself for more than fifteen years, and now I realize that my job is all about teaching and caring for children and their parents, even if they didn't tell me that in college. Even more important, I know that caring for parents in a real partnership is best for children. You may play a role in a child's life for a few years or maybe even up to age eight, but parents play a role in their child's lives forever. It's the job of early childhood professionals to take care of parents too.

Parent Care Is Hard Work

The steps above are simple in theory but are often difficult in practice. With some parents, you will feel the love right away. Others you grow to love, and with some parents, you may not feel that your efforts are even making a difference. You may be asking, "Doesn't a partnership mean two groups of people working together? Doesn't a partnership take two?" And while that statement is essentially true, your job is to help care for and educate parents even if they don't do their fair share in building the relationship. Now, this partnership doesn't sound so simple or fair. You know what your mom told you about life being fair? Seriously, though, parent care doesn't mean that we are going to condone or allow behavior that is inappropriate or hurtful to us or the children. What parent care does mean is that as an early childhood professional, you are going to help parents, even if you don't think that the parents are doing their part by helping you or helping their children in the way you think is best. Why? Because those parents, surprisingly, need your help the most. Why should you care for all parents? Caring for parents is

- good for children
- helpful in making partner-resistant or avoiding parents become better parents
- part of our job
- necessary in today's world, where parents have fewer supportive relationships
- the right thing to do

SELF-ASSESSMENT

How Are You Doing in Caring for Parents?

Take a quick self-assessment to see how you are doing in caring for parents. As you read each of the statements below and circle the frequency that best describes your actions, try to focus on what you can do in creating a real partnership with parents, not what the parents should be doing for you or their children. Be honest with yourself. Understanding your current attitudes and actions toward parents is the starting point for improving your parent care and creating real partnerships.

1 I know the names of each parent in my class.

Always Usually Sometimes Never

2 I welcome all parents as enthusiastically as their children.

Always Usually Sometimes Never

3 I have a positive individual relationship with each parent.

Always Usually Sometimes Never

4 I realize that caring for each parent helps each child.

Always Usually Sometimes Never

5 I keep all parents informed about their children's experience and the program.

Always Usually Sometimes Never

6 I provide a culture that allows all parents to freely express their questions, ideas, or suggestions.

Always Usually Sometimes Never

7 I would never give up on helping a parent, just as I would never give up on helping a child.

Always Usually Sometimes Never

Seven Steps to Partnering with Families

Even if you circled "Always," be sure to read the corresponding step—there's always something to learn and improve on. Refer back to your completed self-assessment form as you explore the seven steps in creating a winning partnership. You will be reminded about each self-assessment statement at the beginning of each step. Don't become discouraged if you don't know as much as you thought you would or should. That's the point. Learning is a lifelong process.

STEP 1

Know the Name of Each Parent

1

I know the names of each parent in my class.

- Always
- Usually
- Sometimes
- Never

Do you know the names of both parents of each child in your classroom? Make a list of all the children and their parents' names.

Child's name	Parents' names

How Many Names Do You Know?

How many names do you need to learn? Some people remember names very easily and others must work at learning names. I am assuming that you know the names of the kids you teach, because "Hey, kid" just doesn't work. And as humorous as that example may be, it's not funny when you don't know the names of the parents you care for. Think about how good it feels when your hairdresser or doctor or someone from the bank knows your name. Calling someone by name is the first step in establishing a real partnership.

In early childhood education, many people tend to call parents by the name of "Mom," "Dad," or nothing at all. Know the voice inflection people use to say hello when they have forgotten your name? They say, "Hi," in that much-emphasized way that really says, "I don't know your name." And then there's the people whom we have been saying hello to for years and still don't know their names, and so much time has passed that it's really embarrassing to even ask their names at that point. Well, as an early childhood professional, you do have to know the names of every parent. Here's a plan for learning those names:

- Make a list of each child and the names of the parents or other guardians who come to your school on a regular basis.
- Commit to learning the names of each person on that list.
- Try to learn at least two or three names a week until you learn them all.
- Introduce yourself to parents whom you do not know and ask their names.
- After you have learned the names of the parents in your class, start to learn the names of the parents whom you often see from other classes.

Look back over your list. Do you know the names of the parents with whom you generally get along well? That's usually the case. You have to work harder to establish relationships with some parents, and you can start by knowing and using their names. Some programs call the parents *Mr.* or *Mrs.*, and in other schools they use first names. Either is fine. Go with the culture your center promotes and the parents' preference.

Do You Love All the Parents the Same?

Don't answer that—we know the answer. Think about the parent you love, the one who comes in your classroom each morning with a box of donuts in one hand and a bag of all the necessary kid stuff in the other: diapers, completed forms, a change of seasonally appropriate clothing. This parent even comes early sometimes to pick up his child. Now think about that parent with whom you get along well. Please do not write down any names. It's important to be confidential and professional at all times as you work to enhance and improve your relationships with parents.

As you think about that parent, list below some of the characteristics or actions of the parent who makes getting along so easy.

1 ______________________________

2 ______________________________

3 ______________________________

4 ______________________________

5 ______________________________

You may have written *is easygoing, appreciates what I do, follows the school rules,* or *thinks I'm a good teacher.*

The Hard-to-Love Parents

Now think about the parent who, well, when she's on vacation, that might be when your relationship is at its best. Just like children, some parents are more challenging than others. Again, no names, but what are some of the characteristics or actions of that parent that make getting along with him or her more difficult or challenging?

1 ______________________________

2 ______________________________

3 ______________________________

4 ______________________________

5 ______________________________

Perhaps you wrote *thinks her child is the only one in the school, doesn't seem to care about being a parent*, or *always forgets things*. Here are some of the reasons for those actions. First, most parents are and should be concerned primarily about their child. Second, you don't always know what's going on in the lives of parents, nor do you necessarily need to know. Finally, being a parent is a tough job, and many parents and people in general aren't very organized.

Build a Partnership with Every Parent

Again, I'm not saying that parents don't have legitimate and accountable roles in the partnership of care and education of their child—hey, you need those immunization forms. I'm only saying that you must keep working toward real partnerships with every parent in your program, whether you feel as if they care or not. (The motivation of parents is discussed throughout this book.)

Just as with children, the personality of parents shouldn't affect how you care for them or act toward them. Once again, I am not talking about parents acting inappropriately or being hurtful to you or their children. Instead, I am suggesting that your efforts to help parents don't rest on their efforts to make your life easier. Make sense?

My Hard-to-Love Parent

Here's a story I want to share with you about a parent who was in one of my centers. When I first started my career as a director, fresh out of Bank Street College of Education, not yet thirty, in a big, corporate Taj Mahal center, there was this parent named Debbie. Debbie had what I call the *big syndrome*. Debbie had a big job title, a big fancy car, a big diamond ring, big hair, and big expectations for the center and her kid. The only big thing Debbie didn't have was a big waist. So right from the start, she irritated me, just because of the mere fact of who she was. Debbie had lots of demands. She was a major high-maintenance parent.

Almost every day, she poked her head in my office or grabbed me in the hall with, as she would say, "Just a little suggestion." As I said before, nothing was little with Debbie. Here are some of the things she had concerns about: "The green beans aren't green enough." "Could my child have the front cubbie?" I guessed she thought front was better, kind of like an executive parking space. Debbie thought toddlers could benefit from phonics instruction and that it was never too early to potty train. Yet despite Debbie's multitude of concerns, I managed to respond to her in a patient and professional way. Debbie needed lots of parent care.

Well, one day I heard Debbie's big high heels clicking down the hall and headed straight for my office. As I said, I had always met her "little suggestions" with attention and interest and made changes accordingly. But on that particular day, I just didn't have the patience to deal with her or her ideas. She was probably going to ask for a graph of the staff turnover rate during the past three years or how often we washed the carpets. Anyway, you know what I did? I hid in my office closet amid the construction paper and glue bottles, and I could hear my associate in the outer office say, "Gigi was just here a minute ago." Now, I am not advocating hiding in the closet as a step to a real parent partnership.

As the years passed, I basically forgot all about Debbie except when I used her as an example of vocal parents in my workshops. So listen to this—it's a true story. Many years later, I'm on the soccer field watching my kids practice, my hair in a ponytail, wearing sweatpants, and who comes across the field headed right toward me in high heels? You got it, Debbie. Her hair was still big and her jewelry was still big and her waist was a little bigger, which was nice.

But I had no place to hide, no closet on the soccer field. I thought about the portable toilet, but no. Debbie walked right up to me, and all I could think of was that she had one last complaint or that she wanted that Excel spreadsheet on toddler biting that I had forgotten to give her all those years ago. But you know what Debbie said? "I just want to thank you for being so available and helpful when my child was at your center. You made such a wonderful impression on me, and to this day, I continue to use things you taught me as I raise my children. Your patience and help, even when I was a little demanding, made me a better parent. Thank you for caring for me as much as you did my child."

I stood there in shock, Debbie thanking me, and you know what I said? "Thank you."

winning ways

Knowing the names of each of the parents of the children in your care is the first step to establishing a family partnership. Calling someone by name may not seem that significant until you think of what your relationships with families really mean. Imagine working closely with someone and not knowing her name. That would seem absurd. Yet often you do not know the names of parents even though they trust you to care for and educate their children. I can't think of a relationship outside of my family that could be more important. Step 2 covers the importance of welcoming families.

OPTIMIZE YOUR KNOWLEDGE

1 Why is knowing the **name** of every parent in your classroom important?

2 List several reasons why you should work to develop **a positive relationship** with a parent even if that parent is not willing to work positively with you.

3 Without listing any names, **create a plan** to develop a partnership with a parent with whom you find it difficult to get along.

STEP 2

Welcome Each Parent

2

I welcome all parents as enthusiastically as their children.

- Always
- Usually
- Sometimes
- Never

What Does Welcoming Each Parent Look Like?

Sometimes welcoming the children with an enthusiastic attitude can be challenging. Welcoming each parent every day can be even harder. You may tend to think of welcoming parents as something that occurs only at drop-off time, but welcoming parents is really an atmosphere that you create in the program throughout the day, every day, even before parents enroll their children. Basically, welcoming parents means "I want you to be comfortable when you are here. I want you to know that you are always welcome here."

> ## Parents Welcome Here
>
> **We want you, parents, to know that you are always welcome here. We want you to know that you belong here. We want you to know that we value you as much as your children.**

Okay, who's thinking *ugg*! Do you really want parents around? What about the child who cries when the parent comes and goes and what about the parent who gets in your way? When you work to create a culture that welcomes parents, children learn that parents come and go. They don't cry as often because they understand that their parents will return. Yes, there are certain children and certain developmental phases in which they may have problems separating from their parents multiple times in a day, and you may have to work with the parents to see what is best for their children. A baby who needs to breast-feed and then cries when the mom leaves is hard, but being fed is of greater importance than the fact that the baby cries. In other situations, you may decide to work with the parents so they do not visit throughout the day for a certain period if their child is having a hard time separating. In both cases, you work with the parents to do what is best for each child and parent. You care for parents.

Do Parents Get in the Way?

What about the parent who gets in the way? Do parents really get in the way? Sure, a parent can distract us when we are trying to care for or teach the children, and in that situation, we need to say respectfully, "I'd like to chat with you now, but I need to give all my attention to the children. May I call you later?" Back to the question "Do parents really get in the way?" In any situation, people can only get in the way if there is not a place for them. You need to make your classroom a place for parents.

- A place where parents feel welcome in the school and classroom
- A place where parents can physically put their things while they are in the school
- A place where parents can help you
- A place where parents can participate in the program
- A place where parents are heard
- A place where you act on parents' questions, concerns, and suggestions
- A place where you wish parents were there with you more
- A place where you don't judge parents who can't be with you all the times you want
- A place where you care for parents

A Welcoming Environment Is All the Time

So welcoming the parents means all the time. Think of a person's home you like to go to and where you feel really comfortable. Whose home is it? Write the name on the line below:

____

Take a few minutes right now to think about why you like to go to that person's home and record your answers below.

1 ______________________________

2 ______________________________

3 ______________________________

A Homelike Environment

You may have said that the home is comfortable or that the person listens to you or that it's fun to be there. Most of the things you wrote on your list are exactly the things you should try to accomplish in your program so that parents feel welcome. But your program isn't a home, you might say. But maybe it is or maybe it should be. Think about it: if young children are spending many hours with you, basically many of their childhood hours, then you are a home, in a sense. Shouldn't your program be more homelike? The answer is yes.

Parents Belong in the Classroom

What does it look like when parents belong in the program and you take responsibility for caring for them too? Parents should be encouraged to visit and hang out and take time to play or eat with their children or just listen to you read a story. To make that really happen, you'll have to do a few things:

- Give it a try. Some programs haven't really had parents involved before.
- Relax. Adding parents to the classroom mix may make things a bit more hectic at first, but remember that it's best for the children, and in the long run, it will be easier and better.
- Don't feel intimidated about the parents watching you. They probably feel nervous themselves—if you're relaxed, they'll relax.
- Let parents know how things work. Explain the routine, hand washing, diapering, where to sit and where not to sit, anything that you think is important.
- Show parents where to put their things.
- Explain what their responsibilities are for their child when they are present, like cleaning up after eating or helping their child get on her cot for nap.

- Remind parents about their role in relationship to children other than their own. Do they help wash the hands of other children? That would be nice. Should parents diaper or toilet other children? Probably not, unless you have a parent co-op program.
- Take the lead in establishing the real parent partnership. Relationships take work. That means encouraging and welcoming families every day.

Too Many Parents?

Can there be too many parents in the classroom? Sure—think about school parties where all the parents are encouraged to attend. The room gets crowded, the space feels cramped, and staff and parents aren't always sure who is really looking out for the children. But it's unlikely that by welcoming parents in the program you'll end up with a chaotic party feel. Not all parents can or want to be in the classroom, and allowing parents in at all times usually creates a natural flow. If, however, you do feel at any time that the room has become adult-heavy, here are some ideas to alleviate the problem without diminishing the we-want-parents-to-feel-welcome culture.

- Take some children outside or for a walk through the school. Never leave the parents to supervise children other than their own.
- Respectfully direct parents where to go. For example, "There are a lot of children sitting at this table. You might want to go over to that table, where you will have more room," or "Some children are going to build with blocks here. You can join in the block building or move over to the reading area."
- Meet as a group with all of the parents if the room becomes too packed with teachers and parents. Adult crowding is a great problem to have, because it confirms that you have created an environment in which parents feel welcome. It's a good problem to have!

Are You Prepared?

Whether a child is just visiting your school or plans to enroll, each family needs a warm, reassuring welcome and many "We're glad you're here" reminders. Preparations for the welcome begin long before the family even arrives, and *preparations* is the key word. It's a wonderful feeling when new faces join your program, and it's important to be prepared for each one so you can offer a warm welcome. Isn't that what you want, to help care for and educate as many children and their parents as you can? But at the same time, it can also seem a bit overwhelming. Do you ever hear yourself thinking or even saying, "Where will I put all these children? There aren't enough teachers now. I need more supplies." Your first interaction with a new child and his family is a special opportunity to welcome them. Here's a quick attitude check to see if you really are welcoming. Complete the assessment below:

1 I acknowledge each child and his family.

Ways to accomplish this:

______

Challenges:

______

2 I am sincerely glad that each child and family is here.

Ways to accomplish this:

______

Challenges:

______

3 I want to make everyone feel welcome and comfortable.

Ways to accomplish this:

______

Challenges:

______

4 I will follow up with each child and family to connect and learn about their experience in the program.

Ways to accomplish this:

______

Challenges:

______

5 I want to hear the questions, comments, and suggestions from the parents.

Ways to accomplish this:

______

Challenges:

______

The first time you meet a new family and their subsequent visits are critical in establishing a partnership with them. There will be parents who easily drop off their children and others who can't seem to leave. In either case, it's your responsibility as a teacher to take the lead in welcoming them and their child. While teachers may sometimes feel intimidated by parents—and if you are new, you may not feel confident about your own skills—you need to remember that parents may be equally intimidated by you, the newness of the school, or leaving their child with new people.

How Can You Make Welcoming Each Child and Family Easier?

If you know a child is enrolling, before the child arrives

- assign a specific teacher to that family
- introduce the parents to that teacher, other teachers, and all the school staff
- send a "what to expect on the first day" note
- make a label for the child's coat hook or cubby
- make a welcome sign with the child's and parents' first names and post it prominently

When the child begins

- have extra teachers, if possible, so you can spend time helping the child and parents separate and adjust
- speak to or call the parents to tell them how their child is doing

After the child begins

- put a photograph of the child and parents on the cubby and elsewhere in the room
- send a handwritten note asking the parents how things are going and extending an invitation to talk
- make sure the parents are on the mailing or e-mail list to receive information about what's happening in the school

Supporting Children and Parents through Separations

Although parents should be welcome all day long, separation is often the most difficult time for parents and children and can put a strain on the relationship between early childhood professionals and parents. Many parents already feel guilty about working and leaving their children. Others may be relieved to drop off their children. As a parent, I've felt both ways, and sometimes I've felt guilty about feeling relieved to go to work.

Parents and their children feel most comfortable in an environment that is emotionally safe. One of the simplest but most difficult ways to welcome parents is to eliminate judgmental attitudes. Parents want to feel accepted. Just showing up in the classroom can be a bold step for some parents. They may think, "I don't belong here. I'm not like these other parents. Sometimes I'm not a very good parent." The way you greet the children and how they separate from their parents can often set the tone for the entire day. Here's some information and ideas for helping with separation anxiety.

How the Children Arrive

Some children separate easily from their parents, while others have more difficulty. These patterns of behavior can change based on the child's age, how he feels, what's going on in his life, and even whether he had a good night's sleep. We can all have off days. Typically, a child will be one of the following:

- eager to come in and participate
- a bit hesitant; the child needs some warming-up time to feel comfortable
- convinced she doesn't want to be here and determined that she isn't staying

Look at the three categories listed and think about the children in your classroom. Write the names of children who fit into each group.

Children Who Are Eager to Participate	Children Who Are a Bit Hesitant	Children Who Don't Want to Stay

Think about the children who are a bit hesitant or who have a particularly difficult time separating. Here are some ideas to help these children feel more comfortable. Can you think of others? Please add your ideas to the list below.

- Let the child hold something special from home: a blanket, stuffed animal, small scarf with mother's perfume, laminated picture of the family.
- Have the child look out the window.
- Read a book together.
- Hold and hug the child.
- Make the child your special helper.
- Go for a quick walk outside the classroom with the child if you have enough teachers.

- Get out a special toy like bubbles or playdough.
- ______________________________
- ______________________________
- ______________________________

There are many ways to make parents feel comfortable about your program, and the more comfortable they feel, the more easily they can leave. Sometimes it's not the child who has a difficult time separating: it's the parent. How do you help parents who are having a hard time separating? What do you tell them, and what do you do? Jot down a few thoughts.

____

____

____

____

____

Am I Ready to Help the Children and Parents with Separation Anxiety?

Use the checklist below to see if you are really prepared to give your full attention to parents and children.

____ I have a written curriculum plan for the day and have the materials and equipment to support that plan. (The plan may be environmentally based or an emergent curriculum.)

____ I have toys or activities set out on the tables or floor to spark children's interest and help ease separation anxiety.

____ I arrive at work at least ten minutes before the children are scheduled to arrive or I am scheduled to work.

____ I am prepared to work by having put away my belongings, finished my coffee, gone to the bathroom, washed my hands, and completed my chatting.

____ I wear a name tag.

____ I work with at least one other teacher, when possible, so one of us can greet children and parents and the other can help children find an activity and become settled.

- ____ I am not only physically present but also mentally focused on helping children and their parents.
- ____ I am ready to greet children and parents with enthusiasm and professionalism.
- ____ I am smiling.

The Value of a Smile

Nothing puts parents more at ease, helps establish a relationship, and says, "I'm glad you are here" like a smile. Smile. There is probably not a thing more rewarding to an early childhood educator than the toothless grin of an infant or the "I did it" smile of a preschooler. Children are amazed by the world and the people in it, and that makes them smile. But some of us adults rarely smile, and for many of us, it's uncomfortable to smile. What happened? Did someone tell us our smile is weird or our teeth are crooked, or were we hit too many times with the favorite adult phrase of "What are you smiling at?" Was smiling socialized out of us? Please know it's okay to smile; in fact, smiling is part of being a professional. If you can smile at kids, you can smile at adults. Give it a try. The great thing about a smile is that it brings joy to the person receiving the smile, joy to the person giving the smile, and joy to everyone around. That's easy.

The Difference Between Feelings and Actions

Just like the kids, sometimes you may be eager to work, or a bit hesitant, or perhaps you just don't want to be there. Everyone has those days. But as a professional, you are responsible for sending a welcoming attitude to parents even when you don't feel like it. Imagine the parents arriving in the morning or at another time, and you are just kind of sitting around, acting like you don't want to be there. "Hey, nothing really planned today. I'm kind of out of it. I'm just going to let the kids run around and play. Have a nice day." If you are thinking that, maybe you need a day off. Speak to your supervisor. If you walk around with a somber, doleful appearance or facial expressions and mannerisms that convey frustration and anger, that's not okay. Imagine a parent seeing you and thinking, "Hey, I don't want to leave my child with her. She looks miserable."

So what is the difference between feelings and actions? Feelings are easy to understand, especially happiness. It's the feeling we get from the circumstances around us—the feeling of a job well done, an unexpected present, finding a parking place up front. Happiness comes and goes all day long, depending on what we are experiencing at the moment. And your days can be pretty complicated, working with children and their parents. That's life. Yet it's your responsibility as a professional to express happiness through actions even if you don't feel it. Get the difference? Happiness is a decision or a choice you make, because you are a professional and your job is extremely important.

Smile Even When You Don't Feel Like It

So smile even if you don't feel like it. We've all seen those people who smile continually and always have something positive to say. What are they so happy about? Maybe it comes easily to them, maybe that's their personality, or perhaps they work hard to be professional and welcoming to parents and children. For those of you who don't smile easily, you'll have to work on it. Not a fake cheerful look but an expression of joy or just of simple contentment. Some people might say, "That's just the way I am. I'm not much of a smiler." Yet look at a room full of children and see the spontaneous and frequent smiles. You were a child once too. Did you grow out of smiling? Did someone teach you to be quiet and serious? Sure, there are times for that, but not when you are welcoming families. So even if smiling doesn't come naturally to you or you don't feel like it, smile anyway, and the good feelings will usually follow.

winning ways

Simple Drop-Off Activities Children Can Do

- Place a star or sticker on the attendance chart.
- Say hello to a special pet or stuffed animal.
- Put a sticker on their shirt.
- Put a ticket to enter in a special box. Give the children a ticket when they arrive. They exchange their tickets for a peek in the treasure box. Put in a new item each morning.
- Answer a "Yes/No" question of the day on chart paper by recording a check mark or writing their names.

Quick Tips to Separation Success for Parents

Share these ideas with parents who have a hard time separating:

- Be positive. Children sense our anxiety and hesitation.
- Realize it's okay if your child has trouble separating. Most children go through periods of separation anxiety.
- Know it's okay for your child to cry when you leave.
- Say good-bye and go. Try not to linger too long, and never sneak out.
- Tell your child, "I will be back after work," or when you will be back.

A Letter to Parents about Separation

Dear Parents,

Leaving your children in the care of other adults can be difficult. Most children adjust quickly, and although they may be upset when you drop them off, they quickly settle down and enjoy the activities in our school and the company of other children their age.

As parents, we often have a more difficult time letting go than our children. Your child takes his or her cues about "Is it okay for Mommy to leave me?" from you. If you are upset about leaving your child, your child is likely to be upset too. Please help make your child's separation more successful by

- Being positive about the program
- Saying good-bye and leaving quickly or helping your child settle down; we will help you determine what works best for you and your child
- Never sneaking out
- Telling your child when you will be back
- Sometimes letting your child cry; crying is a normal reaction, and young children typically express themselves through crying; for infants and toddlers, it's how they express themselves or "talk"

If your child is extremely upset, we will call you. Don't worry—we promise to take good care of your child.

Sincerely,
Your Child's School

Enthusiastically welcoming children and their families often sets the tone for the day. Although some families may respond more positively to your efforts than others, all parents deserve your best attempt. A smile and a sincere "Hello" are a good start to establishing a relationship and partnering with families. Helping children and their parents deal with separation is also an important transition period. You can play a pivotal role in making that transitional process go more smoothly by using some of the ideas in this section. The sample letter to parents shown on the previous page is about ways to deal with separation anxiety. The letter is available at the Redleaf Press website, www.redleafpress.org. Go to the **Winning Ways for Early Childhood Professionals: Partnering with Families** page to access the PDF for use in your program. Step 3 gives tips on how to develop a relationship with each parent.

OPTIMIZE YOUR KNOWLEDGE

1 Observe a classroom during drop-off, and list some of the effective and supportive ways the staff helps the children to **separate** from their parents.

____

____

____

____

____

____

2 Do you agree that **parents** really belong in the classroom? Why or why not?

3 Describe the difference between feelings and actions and why smiling is important in developing **a better relationship** with families.

STEP 3

Develop an Individual Relationship with Each Parent

3

I have a positive individual relationship with each parent.

- Always
- Usually
- Sometimes
- Never

Parents—Who Are They?

Children are all so different and unpredictable at times. As an early childhood professional, I think that's one of the things you most likely enjoy about your job. You like the fact that children do all kinds of things, say all kinds of things, and are always surprising you. But when it comes to parents, you don't want any surprises. Early childhood professionals seem to lump all parents into this giant category of "they." "If they would just read the handbook." "If they would just follow the center's policies." "If they would just keep their children home when they are sick." "If they would just listen to us." "If they would just appreciate us." Sound familiar?

While there are many similarities among parents and their parenting role, there are differences too. The following is a look at what's the same—and I'm not talking about things like "They are always late," "They never sign up for parent-teacher conferences," and "They don't appreciate us." Those statements just aren't true. "They" aren't always late or all unappreciative. You just can't generalize and lump the actions and personalities of all parents together.

What Makes Parents the Same?

I truly believe that all parents want the best for their children. They share some basic goals for their children, even when they don't always know how to meet those objectives or at times do things that seem counterproductive. Unfortunately, there are a few parents who unintentionally or sometimes intentionally harm their children because of frustration, mental illness, addiction, or their own unresolved childhood issues. (I address this in more detail later in the section.) But for the most part, parents are working hard to do what's right for their children. All parents want

- what is best for their child
- to protect their child
- to provide for their child
- to give their child an education
- their child to be successful in school
- their child to be successful in life
- people to like their child
- people to think that they are good parents
- their child to have self-respect and self-esteem
- their child to be physically healthy
- their child to have friends

Can you think of a few more things all parents have in common? Add your thoughts here:

____

____

What Makes Parents Different?

Even though parents have many similar goals for their children, their means to these goals can be different, and their beliefs and values can also be diverse. Some parents think children will be more successful in school if they do worksheets. Why? Those worksheets are evidence that their children are learning. Some parents think their child shouldn't go out when it's cold. Why? They want to protect their child from getting sick. Here's where it gets even more complicated: What is cold? Cold or too cold to go out depends on a lot of factors like where your school is, where the parents grew up, and how they were parented. Cold in Florida is not the same as cold in Colorado. Now throw in state regulations, children's medical conditions, and your own preferences. That's a lot of factors. So what's the answer? That depends on your program. I write about a "why not" approach to parent care in step 8.

Are you supposed to meet the needs of every parent? That's probably not possible in a group care setting, but you are supposed to try. But what if the beliefs of the program don't fit with the beliefs of the parents? Are you supposed to change, or are they? It's your job as a professional to respect the differences of parents and try to accommodate their requests within the program. Is it you *against* them? Not at all. Parent care means it's you *for* them—the children and their parents.

What are some previous parent values or requests that you adapted to in your program? Did you change your menu to reflect better nutrition and more culturally diverse meals? Did you accommodate a grandparent who wanted to be with her grandchild as the child transitioned into the program? Did you change your hours to reflect the care needs of parents? Did you offer parent-education classes based on the parents' topic preferences?

If you're new to your position or to teaching, what are some things you can think of that you could add to the program? You could also talk with your director to find out what your school is already doing to address the needs of the parents.

Changes you made to your program to reflect the needs of parents:

1 ______________________________

2 ______________________________

3 ______________________________

4 ______________________________

5 ______________________________

How about little things? Did you develop a toilet training chart that protects the privacy of each child's progress so a parent doesn't feel bad that her child is not ready to toilet train? Did you change the way you keep track of pacifiers so you are less likely to lose one? Did you keep track of the photographs that you post in the room so every child is represented equally?

Changes you made in your classroom to meets the needs of parents:

1 ______________________________

2 ______________________________

3 ______________________________

4 ______________________________

5 ______________________________

"Us" and "Them"

Like most people in the early childhood field, I have been an "us," an early childhood professional, and a "them," a parent. As a professional, I'm usually rational, consistent, and solution oriented. But when it comes to my own kids, I can become irrational and emotionally driven. The thought of a conference with my three-year-old's preschool teacher would make my palms sweat. I was convinced that whatever my kid's teacher had to say about the quality of his fingerpainting skills and social interactions on the playground would definitely determine the fate of his Ivy League education.

While my "us" side, the educator, writes parenting articles on topics like discipline, nutrition, and limiting TV viewing, my "them" side, the parent, puts my kids in front of the TV and hurls cookies their way when one of them approaches the computer so I can complete my expert work about parenting. It's much easier to write about parenting than to be a parent.

So in the purest sense, an "us" and a "them" mentality is logical. Both sides, educators and parents, want what is best for children, each working from a different perspective, one more rational ("It's not unusual for toddlers to bite"), one more emotional ("Look at the bite on my daughter's face"). Who's right? To a certain extent, both are. But being right is not your goal. It's your job to care and help parents, because helping the parent helps the child, and that's what you're all about.

When Parents Harm Their Children

Before I write more about developing an individual relationship with parents and how you can work to care for them, I need to address the importance of being an advocate for children. What do you do when you see or suspect that a child in your care is being neglected or abused?

Many programs face issues of child abuse, neglect, and family dysfunction. Parenting is never stress free, and each of us has the capacity to harm a child, whether by acting out in frustration or anger, being overwhelmed by circumstances, or neglecting care. You are required by law to report any instances of suspected abuse or neglect. Reporting abuse or neglect can be a traumatic experience for you and can have potentially huge consequences for the family and the school-parent relationship. Sadness, confusion, anger, fear, and other emotions may cloud your decision, including doubt about whether reporting is best for the child. The school and each early childhood professional must follow the state guidelines. Every program should provide training and have thoughtful procedures in place to ensure children are protected and parents are treated respectfully.

In a situation of child neglect or abuse, parent care is needed more than ever. Your role is to help the parent get the right help and resources to be a good parent. You are an advocate for the child and a support system for the parent. Remember that supporting parents when they make inappropriate decisions, especially in cases of abuse and neglect, does not mean that you condone the behavior. It means you want to help.

This difficult situation is the ultimate test of the real partnership between parent and program. If you have a strong bond and mutual trust, there is hope of maintaining the relationship and continuing to support the child and family. Setting boundaries and seeking help for parents are sometimes the best care you can give them.

Reread your state and center policies on reporting suspected child abuse or neglect and sign and date below.

I have read our state and program policies on reporting suspected child abuse.

____

SIGNATURE DATE

Beyond Diversity: Inclusion

Janet Gonzalez-Mena and other respected leaders in early childhood education have taught how important it is to appreciate and celebrate the diversity of others. A lot of progress has occurred in early childhood programs. Most schools have baby dolls with various skin tones in the housekeeping area, musical instruments from around the world, and photographs on the walls that depict the richness of our society. But does your program really reflect the many cultures of children and their parents? To really embrace diversity, you have to live it. Most days, the smell of chicken fingers fills the air in centers. School menus need to include Asian, Latin, and traditional American food. The walls should be decorated with the art and tapestries of your center's families. The program's practices need to validate cultural differences, such as the right age for toilet training and how often infants are held. True diversity is the inclusion of the cultural practices of the families who attend your program. Is your program caring for parents and their children based on their cultural differences? You should know the practices of families represented. List some of the cultural values or beliefs that families in your program have.

____

____

____

10 Ways to Develop an Individual Relationship with Each Parent

1 *Expect relationships to be different.* Some parents want to interact a lot with you, and others maintain a greater distance and seek fewer details about care and education. With my first child, I wanted to know if she got a paper cut. By my fourth child, I didn't need or want much information or reassurance from the program unless he was headed to the hospital.

2 *Ask parents what is important to them.* How do you know if a parent needs little relational contact beyond exchange of pleasantries and relevant care and education information or is too shy or afraid to ask? You ask. Ask parents when their child enters your program or moves to a new room what's important to them. Questions like "Do you need to leave quickly in the morning or can you stay a bit?" "I will call you if your child is sick or hurt, but are there other things that are important to you that I should inform you about before you arrive for pickup?"

What are some things that are important to parents in your care? Write them here.

____

____

____

____

Opportunities to Ask Parents What's Important to Them

When parents

- tour the school
- enroll in the program
- have their child transition to a new classroom
- have a parent-teacher conference
- experience a life change, such as new sibling, home, or job
- learn their child has a new medical condition

3 Don't judge the parent's parenting ability by their relationship with you. It's easy to think that those parents who attend every workshop or social function your program has to offer and spend time chatting with you are better parents than the ones who maintain their distance and seem uninterested. Yes, it is good for children to have their parents participate in school events, but sometimes job constraints or parents' energy levels may keep them from being present. That doesn't necessarily mean that they aren't good parents or don't care.

4 Talk about their child. All parents want to hear positive things about their child. The easiest way to develop a relationship with parents, whether they are close or distant, shy or outgoing, is to talk about their children. Share something their children said or did. Let the parents know you notice the positive qualities in their children.

5 Work on individual parent relationships. Every type of relationship takes work. Notice the types of things that the parent appreciates, such as voice mails, texts, tweets, special notes, or reminders about bringing in supplies, and continue those efforts.

6 Give more to the relationship than you expect to receive. Your efforts to develop an individual relationship with each parent may create mutually beneficial bonds between parent and teacher, but it is unlikely that you will experience a personally rewarding relationship with each parent. As humans, we are drawn to certain people and have more difficulty working with others. As a professional, you must try to develop a relationship, even if the parent does not respond. That does not mean that parents can treat you poorly or neglect their program responsibilities.

Without mentioning the name, write about a parent with whom you had a rough start developing a relationship and with whom you are now making progress or have a good partnership. If you are new to teaching, write about any relationship that's taken time to develop and the things you did to enhance that relationship.

____

____

____

7 **Help even when you don't feel like it.** Some parents are just easier to love and help than others. Some parents are critical of you and the program, demanding, and uncooperative. Those are the parents who need you the most. Keep working on those relationships—if anything, they are opportunities to hone your own relationship-building skills.

8 **Ask the parents questions.** Developing a relationship means understanding the needs of another person and responding to them. It's difficult to anticipate what each parent wants or needs. The best way to do that is to ask. "What else can I do to help you?" It's a good start. Thinking "I must be crazy and parents are going to be impossible?" Unlikely, but that also depends on what you mean by impossible. Asking you to change their child into new clothes before pickup or to feed the child an extra snack might not be impossible.

9 **Don't take things personally.** People who care for young children are usually quite loving and supportive, and that's a good thing. It's also easy to be overly sensitive to the comments and requests of parents. Try not to take things personally when parents don't respond as you want or make comments suggesting that they don't think you are doing a good job. It certainly feels good when parents appreciate your efforts and applaud your work, but keep in mind that you are working for the parent to help the child.

10 **Be a professional.** Early childhood educators should always look for ways to put parents at ease. Parents should feel welcomed and comfortable with the relationship they have defined and confident that you really do want to hear what they have to say.

Positive Parent Conversation Starters

- Your child is so smart. Let me tell you what I saw him do today . . .
- Your child works so hard. Today she was trying to . . .
- Your child is a good friend to others. I watched him . . .
- Your child said something clever. She said . . .
- Your child will make you so proud. Today he . . .
- Your child loves you so much. She told me . . .

Creating individual relationships with families starts by getting to know each family member, and that takes time. When you respect each adult, even the ones who are easy to judge and hard to get along with, good relationships develop. Focus on their perspective, and share your own in a sensitive way. Think creatively about how you can appreciate all family members and their points of view. You'll be surprised how most parents become your ally. You both want the same thing: good care and education for the child. The next step explains why caring for the parent ***is*** caring for the child.

OPTIMIZE YOUR KNOWLEDGE

1 What **surprises** you most about the majority of your relationships with parents?

2 Describe **what you would do** if you suspected someone was harming or neglecting a child.

3 Why do you think teachers take the comments of parents, whether favorable or unfavorable, so **personally?** What is the benefit to you in not taking critical or seemingly critical comments personally?

STEP 4

Care for the Parent to Help the Child

4

I realize that caring for each parent helps each child.

- Always
- Usually
- Sometimes
- Never

Become an Early Parenthood Professional

Taking care of young children seems like enough of a job; taking care of their parents sounds impossible. Are you thinking, "I'm an early childhood professional, not an early parenthood professional?" And why should you take care of parents? It's good customer service, for one, but beyond that, caring for parents promotes better parenting, and that helps the child. Why not soothe a frazzled parent with coffee to go after drop-off or have a place in each room where parents can put down their things while they settle in their child? Offer workshops based on parents' interests. Limit the paperwork that goes home. Plan a school party for which parents don't have to bring anything. Make parking convenient. Send cards to parents for their birthday, promotion, new home, or new child. Have extra diapers, extra milk, and extra bread on hand, so parents can skip a trip to the store. For parents who are occasionally late, feed their children dinner. Yes, that's parent care, and it may make your job more complicated at times, but it's worth the effort. You want parents to succeed so that their children succeed too. Everyone can use a little help, especially busy parents.

Positive Comments to Put Parents at Ease

- It's normal for children to not want to go home at the end of the day. She loves you best, even though it might not seem like it right now.
- Children usually act up more around their parents than in front of others. It can be embarrassing, but don't worry.
- Parenting can be so stressful. We all have hard days. What can I do to help you?
- Balancing work and family is a hard job. We're here to make it easier.
- Organizing all your child's things is a big job. May I help you get her things together?

From Early Childhood Professional to Parent: My Story

It's not necessary to be a parent to be good with parents or their children, but for me, a little real-life parenting really opened my eyes. Before having my own four children, I had many jobs in the early childhood field—toddler teacher, director, toilet plunger—and I willingly, often without solicitation, distributed expert advice to parents across the country, offering tips about how to put their children to bed, the best way to potty train, and why worksheets are taboo. Currently, I'm on a quest to retrace my early childhood encounters, seeking out and apologizing to every parent I ever gave professional advice to.

Why? Hey, some of the advice was pretty good, but what I never delivered with the directions for tantrum-prone kids or the ideas for children who wouldn't stay in bed was sympathy, reassurance, and understanding. I stood on my developmentally appropriate soapbox with an indignant attitude of child-rearing superiority. I made parents feel like failures with my any-idiot-can-do-this expert attitude, and I made hard-working moms and dads who were trying to juggle kids and the bills feel guilty. It wasn't my intention. I just never understood the day-to-day realities of being a parent.

Everyday Parenting

Now in the throes of everyday parenting and moving at mommy hyperspeed, I'll confess that what I say to parents and what I do as a parent can be two very different things. Here are a few examples:

Advice: Ignore fellow shoppers when your child is having a tantrum in a store.
Reality: I ran my credit card to the limit plucking things off the shelves in an attempt to find something to soothe my savage toddler—anything to help him be quiet.

Advice: Please label all your child's belongings, including socks.
Reality: Ever try to label an infant's sock? It's not big enough to write her name on. I was just not up to sewing labels in socks small enough to fit a baby doll.

Advice: Kiss your child good-bye, reassure him that you will be back later, and leave quickly.
Reality: I was either sneaking out or staying until he stopped crying, which was probably around lunchtime. Separation was hard for me too.

Advice: Children learn through play.
Reality: I wasn't sure I wanted to pay all that tuition for my kid to play all day. When was he going to learn to read?

Advice: Childhood is a journey, not a race.
Reality: We may not like it or agree with it, but today's world is really competitive. I want my child to finish the journey in first place.

Advice: Children who wear pull-ups instead of underwear may not toilet train as quickly.
Reality: That may be true, but pull-ups are a lot less messy. For the commute home, I'd put pull-ups on the whole family if they made them big enough for everyone.

Advice: Try to have your child to school on time to avoid disrupting her schedule and the school's activities.
Reality: It wasn't my intention to run my panty hose, run out of gas, or run off the road because of the constant bickering in the backseat. I was always running late.

Advice: Children must be fever free for 24 hours before returning to child care.
Reality: Is that with medication or without? I preferred *with*.

Beyond a Partnership: Parent Care

What's best for the child? You know the answer: a constant eye on caring for the parent as well as the child and an alliance between the parent and the early childhood professional. This means the "us" and the "them" work together, share information, and make joint decisions to determine the individual care and education of each child. But you do that, right? You try, but my guess is your parent partnerships are often no more than cupcakes and fundraisers—opportunities for parents to raise money for the playground or organize teacher-appreciation luncheons. Which are not bad things. But a real parent partnership requires you to listen to the advice of parents, not just for parents to listen to your advice. A real parent partnership comes when you really believe that helping the parent helps the child. Face it: most teachers like well-behaved, quiet parents and their well-behaved, quiet kids.

Some Parents Don't Seem to Care

It's hard to love every child and even more difficult to love every parent. With the hurried lives of some parents, it's easy to wonder, "Why did they have children, anyway?" I knew a parent who took a sales job and hardly saw his children. The wife was like a single mother. The father was always working and spent little time with his children. It was easy for me to judge his parenting as uncaring. I found out later that that dad grew up very poor and was determined to give his children a college education. That dad was my dad, and all three of us, his children, finished college.

How little you know about the lives of the parents who come through your doors! Good programs have learned to tolerate seemingly inappropriate parental ways, such as parents who spend too many hours on the job. But can you learn to accept parents knowing that the majority of them work very hard to make a better life for their children? Can you help parents to help their children?

The Benefits of Parent Care

Perhaps you're still a bit hesitant about all this caring for and helping parents. Does it really matter, or is it just more work to care for parents too? The following are some of the benefits for children, parents, and you. Yes, establishing a real parent partnership helps you too.

The Benefits of Parent Care for Children

- Children, even infants, feel most comfortable in environments where adults work together. Conversely, children also sense conflict and disconnect. They experience stress in situations in which the adults who care for them are not getting along or are not working well together.
- Children see how adults get along and reach resolution when they have differences of opinion. Role-modeling is the greatest form of teaching. You can say "Be nice to your friends," but do you really embrace and demonstrate that to the children by the way you treat the parents in your programs? I'm not saying you should be friends with the parents; I'm just saying you should start at nice and go well beyond that.
- Children receive more consistent care when parents and teachers share information that the teachers use to create individualized routines for those kids. In most situations, teachers expect the parents and children to fit "us" and our way of doing things.
- Children benefit from greater continuity of care between program and home.
- Children benefit from parents who are respected and empowered in their role. When parents feel good about parenting, they feel more attached to their children.
- Children have two groups advocating and working for their best care and education: "us" and "them" are both focused on the child, not on each other.

What are some additional ways that parent care benefits the children?

1 ______________________________

2 ______________________________

3 ______________________________

The Benefits of Parent Care for Parents

Of course the parents are going to benefit—this is all about parent care. Remember the story in step 1 about Debbie and all her demands? Years later, when early childhood professionals and I were no longer even a part of her life, Debbie was benefiting from our deliberate and consistent care, and so were her children. Probably even Debbie's grandchildren will benefit one day, because people tend to parent based on how they were parented. All that from caring for parents? Yes. You have an opportunity to even influence future generations. So how do the parents benefit?

- Parents develop greater confidence in their decision to use care and in their parenting skills. When parents feel confident about their role, they are likely to make better choices.
- Parents aren't alone in raising their children. In today's world, with both parents working, single-parent homes, and transient families, parents don't always have relatives or neighbors to support and help them. In a real parent partnership, you become that community of support—a neighbor in a sense.
- Parents have a voice in their children's care and education, even though they are not with their children all day.
- Parents have people—that's you and your colleagues—who listen to them, respect them, and want them to succeed. Parents need advocates as much as their children do. We can all use someone to listen to us.
- Parents feel less guilty about leaving their child, because they have a voice in their child's care and feel respected.
- Parents feel increased attachment to their children and feel reassured that their children love them best, even though they may spend a great deal of time with you.
- Parents benefit from your expertise and your perspective on their children. You don't always know everything, but you do know a lot about child development and their particular child. You should share this information in a way that empowers and helps the parent, not in a way that makes them feel incompetent and clueless.

What are some other ways that parent care benefits the parents?

1 ____

2 ____

3 ____

The Benefits of Parent Care for Early Childhood Professionals

It's not what you get out of your relationship with parents that should be the motivating factor in establishing and maintaining real parent partnerships. Hey, it's your job to work with children and their families. But you benefit too.

- Teachers have a sense of knowing that they are doing what is right and what is best. We can't put a price on that, even if we could all use a little more money, especially in this field.
- Teachers become more understanding and compassionate about the role of parents and the stresses on families.
- Teachers learn important information about the children from their parents, and doing so helps the early childhood professional become more effective.
- Teachers benefit from the help of parents and their contributions to the program. Baking cupcakes, raising money, and throwing staff-appreciation lunches are all good things.
- Teachers hear parents' affirmations about their work and thankfulness for a job well done. Not all parents will thank you with gifts, cards, or even words. Some parents may not recognize your efforts and how hard your job is until long after they leave the program. Some parents may never understand what you do, appreciate your efforts, or thank you. That's okay too. Most parents will.
- Teachers have the undeniable satisfaction of knowing that they are making a lasting, positive difference in the parent's and the child's lives. That's why most of us are in this field. We really do make a difference.

winning ways

Being a parent is no easy job. Besides caring for their children, they have work, bills, household responsibilities, and more. When you work with young children, you learn that although child care is rewarding, it is also exhausting. Parents feel the exhaustion, too, and many often feel overwhelmed and defeated by so many responsibilities. You see firsthand how parents struggle. You can help parents by committing to provide parent care, not just child care. Children and their families need an advocate in this very demanding world. You can be that person. Read on to learn about keeping parents informed in step 5.

OPTIMIZE YOUR KNOWLEDGE

1 Write about a time when a parent **thanked you** and you didn't expect it. What happened? What did the parent say?

____

____

____

____

____

____

2 Write about a time when after all your efforts, a parent still **wasn't satisfied** and never thanked you. Remember not to list any names. How did you feel?

____

____

____

____

____

____

3 Even though the parent may not have appreciated your efforts, what difference did you make in the lives of the child and the parents? **That's what's important.** List the impact you made. By the way, I thank you.

____

____

____

____

____

STEP 5

Keep Each Parent Informed

5

I keep all parents informed about their child's experience and the program.

- Always
- Usually
- Sometimes
- Never

Keeping Parents Informed: Everyday Communication

The success of every relationship depends upon good communication and lots of it. What you say is not always what others hear. A lot happens each day in an early childhood classroom. Children grow, change, and do amazing things, some good, some not so good. You create new ways of doing things, better systems and procedures, and new policies. With all that going on, how do you ensure that parents, your real partners, know what takes place in your program? It's your responsibility to make sure the parents know what's going on in the school:

- with their child
- in their child's classroom
- in the program

Good communication, verbal and written, and varied methods of communicating the same information are essential to maintain and strengthen your partnerships. How can you create a good system of communication? Look at the list of 9 Ways to Keep Parents Informed and put a check by each method you use to communicate to parents in your school. In the blank spaces, add other ways that you share information.

9 Ways to Keep Parents Informed

1 *Pre-Enrollment Information*

- Brochures
- Business Cards
- School Fact Sheets
- Method for Handling Telephone Inquiries
- Tours
- ______________________________
- ______________________________

2 *Enrollment Information*

- Enrollment Forms
- Initial Parent-Director Meeting
- Initial Parent-Teacher Meeting
- Initial Child-Teacher Meeting
- Parent Handbook
- First-Day Lists
- Family and Child Information
- Short Bios and Photos of Child's Teachers
- ______________________________
- ______________________________

3 *First Day Success Information*

- E-mail or Text or Tweet to Parent After Drop-Off
- Written Note for Child to Read When She Is Older
- Written Note to Parent at Pickup
- Photos of First-Day Experience
- ______________________________
- ______________________________

4 ***Everyday Communication***

- Daily Experience Sheet about Child
- Curriculum Plan
- Highlights of Day
- Medication Administered Form
- Injury or Incident Form
- Minor "Ouch" Forms
- Special News about Each Child
- ______________________________
- ______________________________

5 ***Keeping in Touch***

- Center Newsletters
- Classroom Newsletter
- Telephones Calls
- E-mail
- Text
- Website
- Tweets
- Facebook
- Classroom Monitors
- Calendar of Events
- Menus
- ______________________________
- ______________________________

6 ***Parent Education Programs***

7 ***Parent-Teacher Conferences***

- Conference Forms
- Child Assessment by Teacher
- Child Assessment by Parent
- Child Portfolio
- ______________________________
- ______________________________

8 ***Transitioning to a New Classroom***

- Teachers' Bios
- Tell Us about Your Child Form
- Daily Schedule
- Curriculum Goals
- ____________________
- ____________________

9 ***Special Activities***

- Field Trips
- Back-to-School Events
- Holiday Celebrations
- Graduations
- Birthdays
- Week of the Young Child
- ____________________
- ____________________

Too Much Information?

That's a lot of ways to communicate. It's true, but if you look over the list, what would you eliminate? It's unlikely that there is anything on the list that you would say is not necessary. Your challenge is to provide this information to parents in a systematic, regular way that does not compromise the time you spend interacting with the children and their parents. You don't want to spend more time writing about experiences than having experiences. It's the quality of your communication, not the volume, that really counts.

They Don't Read It Anyway

It's easy to say that parents don't really read it. Some parents don't, and you've probably seen a few parents grab communication from their child's cubbie and toss it without even a glance. But that's not the norm. Some parents save every Daily Experience Sheet that you write about their child and put them in a big scrapbook. That's not the norm, either. Most parents read most of the information you send out. It's your job to share it, and it's the parent's responsibility to be informed about the program. Sure, a great deal of work goes into communicating well to parents.

Communicate Lots of Information in Many Ways

Varied methods of communication serve as reminders to families and appeal to each parent's learning styles. Remind parents too. Oh, yes. How many times have you walked into your kitchen or another room of your home only to ask, "Why am I here?" You forget, and so do parents. How about leaving your wallet somewhere or forgetting to pick up an item on your grocery list? Parents need gentle reminders, and it's your job to provide them.

Communication Is a Two-Way Street

The easiest part of your job in communicating to parents is getting the information out there, but real communication, as with real partnerships, is not just about "us" telling "them" what to do and "them," the parents, doing it. Real partnership communication is about creating a culture in which parents feel invited and empowered to share their ideas and suggestions and in which you act upon them. More information on creating a culture that allows each parent to freely express his or her questions, ideas, or suggestions is discussed in step 6.

Communication Begins Before the Parents Even Enroll

How do you keep parents informed, involved, and educated? From initial school inquiries and first-day successes to parent workshops and ongoing reminders, you can make everyday communication easier. You have an incredible opportunity to begin communicating information about your program to parents before they even enroll. You can use

- Websites
- Brochures
- Business cards
- Fact sheets
- Telephone inquiries
- Tours

How do you think most parents find out about your program? ____________

____

Where do parents get their initial information? ____________________

____

How do you encourage parents to learn more about your program? ________

____

How to Start That Real Partnership from Day One: Show Off Your Program to Prospective Parents

- Give them an awesome tour.
- Highlight the features in your program that set it apart from other programs.
- Have printed materials to give the parents.
- Share quotes from current parents.
- Provide prospective parents with contact information for a current parent who is willing to talk with them.
- Develop a scrapbook of field trips and center events.
- Let them see the kids and teachers in action.
- Describe staff training opportunities.
- Keep newspaper clips about the school.
- Frame and hang awards and certificates. Too many certificates? Start a scrapbook.
- Point out teachers' biographies.
- Bake cookies so your center smells good.
- Call the parents after the tour and ask them what they thought.

Are You Ready for Prospective Parents to Tour Your Center?

1. Know what you are going to say. Create a fact sheet with the features of your program you want to highlight and show those to the parents.
2. Prepare by giving your program a sniff test. When you live or work in a place, you become so familiar with your surroundings that you often forget what they look or smell like to others. Ever enter your house after being away on a vacation and think, "What is that smell?" That's how your house smells. And that smell can be good or not so good. The same goes for your program. Ask yourself these questions:
   - What does it look like? Cluttered or clean?
   - What does it smell like?
   - How does it sound?
3. Listen to the prospective parents. What are their questions? What are their concerns?
4. Be honest. In a good program, you don't need to hide the limitations of group care, the struggles to produce quality with limited resources, or pretend to be something you are not. If you lead parents to expect something you can't deliver, you will have serious problems after they enroll.

5. Involve everyone in the tour's progress. The tour guide should introduce staff, saying something positive about each teacher the parents meet.
6. Express your interest to the parents and child about having a new family in their program.
7. Call the parents after the tour to see what they thought.

Beginning a Partnership in the Enrollment Process

Once parents make a decision to enroll in your program, the real partnership begins. Your responsibility is to make enrollment and settling in positive processes for both parent and child. How can you make enrollment easier for parents? Start by caring for them right from the beginning. Ever try to fill out your own enrollment forms? Most forms don't have a space large enough to write the asked-for information. Try placing your forms online, so parents can complete and e-mail them. For parents who don't use computers, can't read, or have a language barrier, sit with them, ask the questions, and fill out the form for them.

What Parents Need to Know During the Enrollment Process

Communication is ongoing, and so is reminding parents about information you have already shared. Although you give them a great deal of information during the enrollment process, parents don't always tune in to the specifics until they become involved in a particular situation. You can explain how you deal with biting during the enrollment meeting, at Back-to-School Night, even during a parent workshop, but it's not until their child receives a bite or gives a bite that they really use and internalize that information. Think about it: you may be given an overview of a hotel, but you aren't likely to think about where the pool is until you are looking for it. Or this: you get a new cell phone and you read through the instructions, but it's not until you actually need to create your voice-mail message that you refer to the section on how to make a greeting. Make sense? You live in the early childhood world and have become so familiar with it that at times you can forget others, especially parents, don't have your perspective. So what do you do?

- Provide parents with the information they need.
- Expect parents to read the information but know that some won't.
- Remind parents about things to do, like completing forms or bringing in supplies.
- Highlight sensitive issues like biting, but expect that parents may still be upset when the situations occur.

- Make all communication, whether verbal or written, professional.
- Question how effective your communication is.

Think of Ways to Improve Your Communication

Write about a time when you thought that you had communicated well to parents, but they didn't understand you or respond as you anticipated. Remember: no names.

____

____

____

____

What could you have done differently to improve the communication?

____

____

____

____

What Should Parents Learn about During the Enrollment Process?

- who their child's teachers are and how the room is staffed
- the daily routine of their child's classroom
- how the program handles discipline
- what type of curriculum you have
- how your learning environment is set up
- what to do when their child is sick or needs medication
- overview of sensitive issues, such as biting, special needs, or behavioral challenges
- what you expect from the parents and what they can expect from you

Keeping Parents Informed about Their Child

Some parents will read everything you send out and even try to catch a glimpse of what you send out to other parents, but in most situations, parents are most interested in information that directly affects their child. "How is my kid doing?" "Is my kid smart?" "Is my child growing and learning like other children?" The best way to address these concerns is through daily written information. You can't always talk to parents at the end of the day, because you are still supervising other children or you may not want to discuss certain topics in front of the child.

Who's Got Time to Write about Every Child?

Balancing caring for and educating children with writing about that experience is difficult for teachers. Here are some tips to make completing daily sheets more effective:

- Create a form that works for the ages of the children, your program, and parents' preferences.
- Have all the teachers help complete the daily sheets.
- Complete the experience forms as the day progresses. (If you are writing the information on one sheet and then rewriting it on your form, your form is not effective.)
- Ask each parent what information is important to them. Include that information on the form.
- Write a specific sentence about a child's experience, not a general statement. "Louie built a castle in the sandbox and decorated it with small rocks" is more interesting to a parent than "We went outside to play."

Daily Experience Sheets

Daily written information is not meant to take the place of having real conversations with parents or telling them sensitive information, such as "Your child is very aggressive in school, and we need to have a meeting." While you may want to say that and writing it may seem easier than facing the parent, daily sheets are intended to let parents know what happened in their child's day. What you write should be positive, but honest and accurate. What if a child did push? What do you write? You write, "Sam was frustrated in the block area today and pushed a friend instead of using his words. We talked about it, and he said he would come get me next time."

As a parent, I know what it's like to get a note about my child not behaving well—it feels horrible. Parents feel like their child is destined for *America's Most Wanted*. At the same time, you do have to share information with parents that helps them learn about their child's experience. A well-written note or journal entry demonstrates that their child is noticed, well cared for, and appreciated. In writing daily sheets, try to give an accurate sense of the child's day without sugar coating it or making the parents feel bad. Always include positive information that will make parents feel happy about their child's experience. The daily experience sheet that's featured here is available at the Redleaf Press website, www.redleafpress.org. Go to the *Winning Ways for Early Childhood Professionals: Partnering with Families* page to access the PDF for use in your program.

Daily Experience Sheet

Child's Name: Today's Date:

Parent Information

Where can we reach you today? Please list place and telephone number.

____

How did your child sleep last night? ________________

What time did your child wake up? ________________

What kind of mood is your child experiencing? ____________

What time will your child be picked up? _______________

By whom? ______________________________

Did your child have any medication today? ______________

If, yes, what and when? ______________________

Does your child have any injuries or symptoms of illness? ________

____

Are there any circumstances at home we should be aware of? ______

____

Do you have any special instructions or information? _________

____

Teacher Information

Your child ate: ___________________________

____

Your child napped: _________________________

If medication was given, list name, time, and dosage.

____

Today your child: __________________________

____

____

Please bring in: ___________________________

Just a reminder that: ________________________

Daily Sheet Starters

Your child (use the child's name):

- Told me . . .
- Made a . . .
- Helped by . . .
- Told a friend . . .
- Did . . . all by himself
- Made me laugh by . . .
- Learned a new skill . . .

What to Do with Difficult Communication

At times, a child's behavior or growth and development may concern you. Sometimes developmental delays or behavioral problems are not evident to a child's parents or pediatrician. Before communicating sensitive and potentially partnership-compromising information to parents, you need to be confident that your concerns are valid. How do you know if a child needs help beyond what you can provide or if she simply annoys you? Take a look at the following ideas and questions:

- Do you have a concern that a child may have a condition that is atypical?
- Do you think a child may benefit from early recognition and intervention?
- What behavior or absence of behavior concerns you? Describe it in detail.
- Document your concerns. Describe the behavior. Indicate the situation(s) in which it happens. Note the date and time.
- Compare the child's behavior or absence of behavior to developmental norms. Most child care teachers are not trained to assess children, so your conclusions are merely observations.

- Bring the concern to the attention of your supervisor.
- Respect the child and family by maintaining confidentiality and limiting conversations with other staff unless it concerns them.
- Share your concerns with the parents and be prepared for an emotional response, denial, or deflection of the issue back on you or the program.
- Develop a plan for further observation.
- Direct the parents to consult outside resources or get permission from the parents to contact resources yourself.
- Learn how to better assist the child in your environment.
- Celebrate the successes and abilities of the child.

Sharing a Child's Behavior with Parents

If you do have documentation that a child may require a specific care or educational strategy or may have needs beyond your expertise, share your concerns with the parents. Providing parent care, just like child care, does not imply that you are a social worker or counselor or that parents should expect such expertise from you. You can provide resources for families of children who require additional services, but trying to provide those services yourself without the training and certification to do so can cause harm. You can provide families with many services within your realm of expertise, given your innovation, desire to enhance the lives of the children and families you serve, and wish to help them.

Before you approach the parents, document or write down the child's behavior to see if changing routines, schedules, or environment will help the child succeed. If you decide to have a conversation with the parents, here are the steps to follow:

1. Make sure that you are objective and not just annoyed with the child.
2. Reassess your expectations to make sure they are developmentally appropriate—the child should be capable of doing what you ask.
3. Talk with a supervisor before approaching the parents.
4. Be positive and look for the strengths and endearing qualities in the child.
5. Ask to speak to the parents in private or make plans for a telephone call. These are not the type of conversations to have around children or other parents.
6. Be clear about what you see the child doing or not doing.

7 Be prepared with specific examples about the child's behavior or absence of behavior and what feelings the child exhibits.
8 Be honest and direct about your concerns or questions while being compassionate and recognizing the parents' sensitivities.
9 Do not judge the child or the parents.
10 Listen to the parents and try to understand their perspective.
11 Expect parents to respond in varying ways: anger, denial, tears.
12 Remember that you are trying to help the child and the parents, and don't take the situation personally.
13 Apologize if you make a mistake or say something incorrectly.
14 Keep the best interests of the child and parents in mind. Let your pride go.

A Little Communication or a Lot of Communication?

You must provide all parents with some information, and some parents want a little more, and some parents want a little less. As a mom of four, my expectations have changed with each child. With my first child, I wanted to know if the teachers changed her clothes and why and what outfit they put on her. I wanted to know if she got a split end or lost the bow in her hair or cried at all. By my fourth, I told the teachers not to call me unless he was headed to the hospital. Did I love the first child better than the last? Not at all—I just got more comfortable with being a parent and much more comfortable and trusting of the program. I had the benefit of all of my children attending the same wonderful program. Can you imagine what a real parent partnership my husband and I had with the program after nine years of having our children in their care? I wonder if they were glad to see us go? Over nine years, we needed a lot of parent care. I'm happy to say we still visit sometimes.

winning ways

Regardless of the many ways you communicate, nothing can take the place of those casual though short chats at drop-off and pickup. Real parent partnerships can be enhanced or compromised during the daily moments of arrival and departure. Each day, you have an opportunity to build the relationship through good communication. Bottom line: talk with the parents. What's the next step? Creating a culture in which parents can share ideas, ask questions, and make suggestions.

OPTIMIZE YOUR KNOWLEDGE

1 Refer to the list 9 Ways to Keep Parents Informed on pages 49–51 and check all the ways that your program **communicates** with families. Circle three ways that you will start using to communicate with families.

2 What do you think most **impresses** prospective parents about your program? What do you think most impresses parents who have been enrolled in your program for at least several months? Are they different or the same?

3 What are the purposes of a **daily experience sheet?**

STEP 6

Create a Culture in Which Parents Can Share Ideas

6

I provide a culture that allows all parents to freely express their questions, ideas, or suggestions.

- Always
- Usually
- Sometimes
- Never

Create a Program Culture That Solicits Parents' Input

How can you give parents an opportunity to influence your program? Ask them. Call a few parents each week just to check on how things are going. Keep a checklist and call every parent at least once during the year. Have handouts of a two-minute survey in the lobby and ask parents to record something they liked recently and something they would like to change. Call parents whose children have graduated from your school and give them the same two-minute survey: "What did you appreciate about the school? Where could we make improvements?" Sound like hard work? It is. Sound like it's good for the children? It is. Is it worth the effort to have the best parent care? It is.

The Parent Is the Customer

As much as parents are your partners, they are also your customers, whether they are paying for early childhood education or receiving it as a public service. It's parent care, and parents are customers. Does thinking about the parent as a customer seem to negate or diminish the importance and seriousness of the social service you provide? You might be thinking "We're caring for children, not selling clothes in a department store or meals in a restaurant." Thinking of parents as customers does not undermine the importance of what you do. To the contrary: seeing parents as customers helps you to focus on how you can improve their experience and their child's. The concept of parent as customer does not in any way undermine your credibility or expertise.

If you were scheduled to have surgery, you would have a lot of questions about the procedure, not because you're the medical expert who can perform the operation but because you are the expert on your body. If you use the premise that parents are the experts on their children, then they really are your customers, and you should treat them as such.

You know the saying "The customer is always right." It's not true. No one is always right. The customer, the parent in this case, is not always right, but you're always listening. Hey, you'd love it if the parents never complained, paid their tuition on time, listened to your advice. It'd be great if they did everything you asked, since you are in fact the expert, but as inconvenient as it may be, you should expect good parents to be demanding, questioning, and involved. Why? It's good for their child.

If the Customer's Not Always Right, How Do You Respond?

If the customer's not always right, how do you respond to their sometimes seemingly unreasonable requests? My friend and mentor Jim Greenman would say, "Answer every parent's request with an attitude of 'Why not?'" The customer service concept of "Why not?" is simple, but it can have a profound impact on your program, your real parent partnerships, and parent care. Here's how it goes. Whenever a parent asks you a question, your first response is "Why not?" Here's what it means. You develop an attitude of being more open minded toward the suggestions, concerns, and questions of parents. You remember that parents are not against "us," but for their children, just as you are. A "Why not?" mind-set toward new ideas and ways of doing things creates a cohesive environment. You and the parents are working together to affect children positively.

Common Responses to Parents' Questions, Suggestions, and Concerns

When you are not working in partnership with parents, you are usually just taking the lead and expecting them to follow. When you work together, you are letting the parents influence your program and even its policies. Little scary? Oh, yeah, but here's the helpful thing about "Why not?" "Why not?" does not always mean "Yes." Even though the customer is not always right, you are always listening. Listen with an open mind so your care and teaching more closely reflect the needs of the parents and their children.

What are you often thinking when parents express suggestions, questions, and concerns? Have you ever thought or said any of the following?

- That's not the way we do it here.
- This is group care, not one-on-one.
- That will never work.
- I'm an early childhood expert, and I know what's best.
- Is this parent crazy?
- Does she think that her kid is the only one I have to watch?
- He has got to be kidding.
- I don't make enough money for that.
- No way.

Come on and admit it—everyone has had those thoughts at times. Unfortunately, you may express them that way at times too. So what do you do to provide good parent care, balance the needs of the each child with the needs of the group, and not go insane? You simply keep an open mind to parents' suggestions, questions, and concerns, and you recognize that improving and enhancing your program is good for everyone.

My "Why Not?" Story

So after hearing all this "Why not?" stuff from Jim, I decided to answer every parent question with the attitude of "Why not?" I was holding on to what seemed like the only sensible part of this customer service approach, which was that "Why not?" does not always mean "Yes." Thank goodness I had this attitude! Remember Debbie? When we were hiring a new teacher for her child's classroom, Debbie asked me, "Can I hire the new toddler teacher?" "Sure, Debbie," I wanted to say, "and you can have my job too." But after I really thought about it, I said, "Why not?" Now, Debbie didn't actually get to hire the teacher, but she did interview the teacher as a parent representative, and I learned so much of what was important from a parent's perspective. Debbie asked questions that were important to her and Debbie also learned about the pool of potential teachers we could draw from, teachers' salary ranges and benefits, and our very thorough process for hiring new teachers. Debbie had a greater appreciation for our job and how we hired new employees. That "Why not?" approach helped us all. I figured if a teacher could survive an interview with Debbie, she would be a good hire.

"Why Not?"—Yes or No?

Your response to a parent's request depends on a number of factors, such as the number of staff you have, their experience and sophistication, your facility and funding, and the nature and time of the request. It may be difficult to meet a request if you have a few teachers to hire or your facility is undergoing construction. But with some creative thinking from teachers and an attitude of "This might not be a bad idea after all," most programs can meet most reasonable parents' requests.

Look at the following parents' requests below. Why do you think the parent is making this suggestion or asking that? Using a "Why not?" customer service approach, how would you respond? Check yes or no, and answer the questions that follow.

1 ***"Can my child stay inside today since she has been sick?"***

How would you respond? ○ Yes ○ No

Why? ____

____

What would you say to the parent? ______________________

____

2 ***"My child is twelve months. It's time to start toilet training."***

How would you respond? ◯ Yes ◯ No

Why? ______________________________

____

What would you say to the parent? ______________________________

____

3 ***"I don't mind if my child gets messy during the day, but can you make sure she has on clean clothes before I pick her up in the evening?"***

How would you respond? ◯ Yes ◯ No

Why? ______________________________

____

What would you say to the parent? ______________________________

____

What's the Right Answer?

What's the right answer to these questions? There's no right answer. But are you ready for my answer? All of these requests came from real parents in real programs in which the early childhood professionals were able to say yes to parents about their child staying inside for a day, toilet training at twelve months, and changing the child's clothes before pickup. The requests were also fulfilled without compromising the safety of the child, developmentally appropriate practice, state regulations, or accreditation standards. I'm not saying your program should say yes to those requests—I'm merely suggesting that it's possible to respond favorably to parents' cultural requests and parents' preferences more often than you may think. There are countless ways to provide more individualized parent care and child care.

What Do Others Think? Active, Hands-on Learning or Just a Messy Child?

If a parent heads to the grocery after picking up her child from school and the child has on dirty clothes, what do you think people in the grocery will think about that mom and her child? It's unlikely that someone will go up to the parent and say, "Wow, you are an amazing parent. I can see from how dirty your child is that you selected a school in which they engage the children in an environmentally based curriculum and the children learn through active, hands-on, messy play. Well done, parent." Probably not. Most people view dirty, disheveled kids as neglected kids. People are more likely to think, "Look at that mom all dressed up and look at her dirty little child. She must care more about herself than her kid." Possible? What do you think?

Name what you considered an unusual or a demanding request from a parent.

____

____

Summarize what you did at the time.

____

____

____

Now that you understand the concept of "Why not?" would you still respond in the same way? Explain.

____

____

____

Parents Are Experts on Their Children

Understandably, parents want control over the care and education their child receives. Parents typically use their financial means to find a program they can afford and trust, one in which they can rely on the professional judgment of the staff for many decisions.

But what if parents don't have money or a clear sense of what is good for their child? Perhaps they have an idea of the type of care they want, but they aren't very articulate, or perhaps it seems as if they don't really care about being parents at all? What then? Are all parents really experts on their children? Yes.

All parents (almost without exception) have an unconditional love for their child that drives them to want their child to succeed and be accepted. It isn't just parents with money who want, need, and deserve involvement in their children's experience and have a right to influence the program. It's most, if not all, parents. It's your responsibility to make all parents feel competent as parents and to involve them in the care of their child, whatever their skills and resources or lack thereof.

What Parents and Teachers Are Thinking about Each Other

All parents feel insecure at times, even if they don't seem to express it. I never thought of demanding Debbie as being insecure. On the contrary, I was insecure, and I thought she had it all together. It's easy for some parents to love the great care you give their children and their children's attachment to you. At the same time, other parents can feel jealous and inadequate when their children seem to be more attached to you or when their children misbehave for them but not for you.

I gave a lot of parent workshops on discipline at my own children's program, and I lived in constant fear that at pickup time, my kid would flip out in the lobby for all to see. Or worse: all of those lame discipline ideas I gave everyone wouldn't work. I wanted people to think I was a good parent. I think sometimes that we early childhood professionals feel intimidated by parents or at odds with them because of our own insecurities. If early childhood professionals started from a position of respect and appreciation from society and ourselves, perhaps we would feel more comfortable in our role with parents.

Teacher Competence and Parent Self-Esteem

The more competent teachers are, the more parents may feel insecure about their own parenting unless priority is given to forming partnerships. Teachers have two somewhat conflicting agendas. First, we want parents to feel secure leaving their children at the program and we want to demonstrate competence and understanding of each child. Second, we want parents to feel important and needed by their children and even by us. It is easy for teachers with good intentions to undermine parents by offering unsolicited advice, describing how the child behaves better at school than at home, or simply by appearing competent and confident when the parent does not. Despite your insecurities or those of the parents, a real partnership depends upon both partners understanding their roles and the responsibilities that go along with them. What should parents expect from you, and what should you expect from parents?

The Roles and Responsibilities of Teachers and Parents

Teachers have a responsibility to

- Encourage parents to visit. Welcome parents at all times, even when it seems inconvenient to you. Be honest about how a parent's visit might affect their child or the program. It's easy to think that parents' visits are disruptive. That's not always true. Most children can easily handle a parent coming and going, especially if that's the norm.
- Share program information. Give parents written materials about policies and procedures: parent handbook, illness information, discipline policy, and other documents you think are important. We all want to know what's expected of us, and parents can't know unless you tell them. The letter shown here is available to download from the Redleaf Press website, www.redleafpress.org. Go to the *Winning Ways for Early Childhood Professionals: Partnering with Families* page to access the PDF files for use in your program.

Dear Families,

We love it when your children attend our program. Many of us are parents ourselves, so we know how difficult it can be when your child is sick. For the protection of the entire group and to reduce the amount of illnesses children pass to one another, we ask that you keep your children home if you notice the following:

- Elevated temperature
- Severe runny nose
- Severe cough
- Mucus that is not clear
- Diarrhea
- Vomiting
- Contagious stage of any disease, like chicken pox or pinkeye
- Behavior indicating pain
- Uncontrollable crying

Thank you for your cooperation,
Your Child's School

- Teach parents about the program. Show them what to do. Written materials are essential, but showing parents how to sign in their child, where to put their and their child's things when they are in the center, and where to park make parents feel more comfortable.
- Tell parents about the staff. Talk up the staff. Post a short bio and photograph for each staff member that describes the teacher's experience, education, credentials, and training. Add some personal information about her family and her hobbies. Parents need to know who is working with their child, and personal information helps to build the relationship.
- Inform parents about teachers' schedules. Tell parents about the staffing patterns, and inform them when there are changes in who is caring for their child.
- Provide detailed daily information to parents about their child. Use daily experience sheets and photographs to capture the child's experience for the parents.
- Create a program culture that solicits parents' ideas and suggestions.
- Maintain confidentiality.
- Support and care for all children and their parents.

winning ways

What to Do with Staff Bios

- Frame a bio and photograph of each staff member and hang them in the lobby.
- Hang another framed bio outside the classroom or the area where they work, such as the kitchen or office.
- Copy the bios and compile a book for the center's lobby.
- Highlight an employee of the week or month.
- Give parents a copy of their teachers' bios when they enroll in the school or transition to a new room.
- List a few details about a teacher and ask the center's parents to guess who the staff member is.
- Update and change the bios often to create new interest.
- Add stickers or a list of new trainings to each bio whenever the teacher completes workshops.
- Have staff answer fun questions about themselves that parents and children will find interesting to read. Examples include "What kind of pet do you have and what is his name?" "What's your favorite kind of ice cream?" "What's the best vacation you have ever had?"

Parents have a right to

- Visit and observe the school
- Be assured of a safe and healthy learning environment for their child
- Ask questions
- Receive information about the program
- Obtain information about their child
- Expect confidentiality

Parents have a responsibility to

- Comply with program policies
- Read school communications
- Provide information essential to caring for their child
- Respect staff as professionals

Parents should be allowed to

- Advocate for their child
- Advise the program about policies and procedures
- Evaluate their experience
- Promote the school

Parents' Rights and Teachers' Responsibilities

Parents' rights and teachers' responsibilities line up perfectly. What parents have a right to expect, you have a responsibility to provide. Take a look.

Teachers have a responsibility to	Parents have a right to
Allow parents to visit at any time.	Visit the school at any time.
Create a safe and healthy learning environment.	Be assured of a safe and healthy learning environment.
Answer parents' questions with a "Why not?" approach.	Ask questions.
Distribute information about the program.	Receive information about the program.
Give information about each child's daily experience.	Obtain information about their child.
Maintain confidentiality.	Expect confidentiality.

Ask Them

How do you know what parents are thinking about their child's experience? Ask them. It's easy to think that if parents aren't saying anything, they don't have any issues. That's not usually true. If you want to know what some parents are thinking, you have to ask. And if you ask, you have to be prepared to listen and—most important—to act on the parents' suggestions by educating them about practices already in place or making changes to enhance or improve your program. Check out the three quick and simple forms that follow to help you find out what parents are thinking. The forms are available at the Redleaf Press website, www.redleafpress.org. Go to the *Winning Ways for Early Childhood Professionals: Partnering with Families* page to access the PDF files for use in your program.

Two-Minute School Survey for Parents

Name (Optional): ______________________________

One thing I love about my child's experience in school is

____

____

____

One thing that the school might want to do or change is

____

____

____

Tell Us What You Think Survey

Tell us what you're thinking about your child's and your experience in our school:

I like . . .

I don't like . . .

I wish . . .

For the next time . . .

It would be great if . . .

Did you ever consider . . .

If I were involved, I would . . .

I want you to know . . .

I had a question about . . .

Annual School Survey

Date: ______________________ Parent's Name (optional): ______________________________

Child's Name (optional): ______________________________ Age of Child: ________________

Please circle the number you feel corresponds to each statement.

5 = Strongly Agree, 4 = Agree, 3 = Somewhat Agree, 2 = Disagree, 1 = Strongly Disagree

1	The atmosphere of the school is warm and friendly.	5	4	3	2	1
2	I feel welcome and comfortable in the program.	5	4	3	2	1
3	The teachers and staff greet my child and me by name.	5	4	3	2	1
4	My child looks forward to coming to the program.	5	4	3	2	1
5	I know my child is safe.	5	4	3	2	1
6	The teachers and staff know my child.	5	4	3	2	1
7	My child is learning to interact with other children.	5	4	3	2	1
8	My child learns.	5	4	3	2	1
9	I feel informed about how my child is doing in school.	5	4	3	2	1
10	I know about program activities and events.	5	4	3	2	1
11	I feel comfortable bringing my concerns to the teachers and staff.	5	4	3	2	1
12	The teachers and staff address my concerns promptly, even if they cannot accommodate my wishes.	5	4	3	2	1
13	I have confidence and trust in the school's leadership.	5	4	3	2	1
14	The environment is clean and organized.	5	4	3	2	1
15	There are adequate supplies and materials in good condition.	5	4	3	2	1

winning ways

When Parents Don't Like What You Do

Sometimes parents are unhappy about the way you do things in the classroom or program, or about an incident, such as biting or a lost personal item. Maybe they don't understand why you do things the way you do, or perhaps they care for their child another way or do things differently at home. There are bound to be differences. Even within the same family, each parent may have a different approach to parenting.

It's not unusual for parents to want you to do things their way, since that's what their child is used to, that's how they were parented, or that's what they believe is best for their child. Parents may also disagree with you about certain rules in your program: how long children should sleep, what to do if they cry, or what constitutes real learning. They may hang on your every word and worry about what a teacher says or has done. Parents may also be upset or even angry about what you say or don't say, or do or don't do. Conflict and misunderstandings are inevitable in any relationship. Parents' and teachers' emotional attachment to and investment in the child often increase tension in early childhood programs. It's not a matter of if parents and teachers disagree but of *how* you handle these disagreements knowing that you both care about the child. So how do you deal with these?

- Be professional.
- Don't take things personally.
- Keep inappropriate conversations away from all children.
- Give parents the benefit of the doubt.
- Listen when the parents are upset.
- See the real issue despite parents' anger or concern.
- Don't hold grudges.
- Clear up the misunderstanding through conversations and action.
- Let it go and move on.
- Concentrate on what's good for the child.
- Think parent care.
- Love the parents even when you don't feel like it.
- Have a "Why not?" attitude.

As an early childhood professional, you are aware that program life is not without real issues, concerns, and honest questioning by families about policies and decisions. It's how you respond to those issues that matters, and more important, how you create a culture that says you want to know what families are thinking and feeling about their experiences in the program, even when what they say is not positive. Your created culture should make a commitment to work through "Why we do things the way we do" and to meet the needs and interests of families with a "Why not?" attitude. It's much easier to tell parents what to do than solicit their thoughts on what you should do. Are you ready to give it a "Why not?" The right thing to do in any difficult situation is not always clear or immediately possible, but you should always be willing to try. *Never Give Up* is the next step to partnering with families.

OPTIMIZE YOUR KNOWLEDGE

1 Explain what the concept **"the parent is the customer"** means to you.

2 Create a **staff bio** for yourself. Write and format it to demonstrate your professional knowledge, experience, and personal information, so families can get to know you better.

3 Give an example of a situation in which the parents or family **didn't agree** with what you did. How did you handle the situation?

STEP 7

Never Give Up on Helping a Family

7

I would never give up on helping an adult family member, just as I would never give up on helping a child.

- Always
- Usually
- Sometimes
- Never

Family Care

Think about the children whom you care for and educate. You would never look at an infant who is struggling with large-motor skills, one who isn't pulling up on things or showing signs of walking, and say, "Don't worry about that child. I don't think that one is likely to walk." You would never say, "That preschooler over there is having a hard time learning new words and never stays focused. He's unlikely to be a good reader." Are you appalled that I would even write those comments about children? Of course you are. Don't all early childhood professionals do everything possible to help children become successful? You begin by assessing whether you are setting the child up to succeed. You ask yourself "Is the environment appropriate?" "Is the routine suitable?" "Am I spending enough time with the child?" "Are my expectations appropriate?" As a good teacher, you document the child's behavior and bring in people to help you. Right? You'd do almost anything to help a child.

Unfortunately, when it comes to adults, especially parents, you tend to give up on them. You judge and blame them. You don't think they care or will ever change. You think, "Why did she have kids?" or "He'll never be a good parent."

If you really want to help the child, you have to really want to help the parent. Challenge yourself to move beyond child care to family care, and never give up on an adult, just as you never give up on a child. Parents are children who are all grown up and just not as cute.

Beyond Child Care: Family Care

Sometimes early childhood professionals assume that those initial efforts of welcoming new families to the program, speaking a few words to each parent every day, and giving families written information are enough to partner with them. But partnering with families requires intentional and consistent energy and effort. Relationship building is a daily process dependent on you, the teacher. You have to show parents every day that you want to have a real partnership with them. That takes work. If teachers and parents do not understand how each other feels, they may misinterpret what is actually a lack of confidence, reading it instead as aloofness or unfriendliness, to the detriment of the relationship. The important thing is to understand issues that parents and families face, so you can care for the children and care for the parents.

Winning ways

Values and beliefs can be found at home and in your programs. You transition from home to work, the children move from home to school, and the parent to work. At the end of the day, everyone heads back home again. It's an often confusing and busy world for everyone involved. The parents need to understand the way the center works, and you can provide better care and education when you understand the parents' views. Understanding happens when you talk to them, exchange information, and have real sympathy for their role. It would be great if they understood and appreciated your role, too, and many parents do. But whether parents embrace you in a more personal partnership or keep a comfortable, yet professional distance, it's up to you to initiate and maintain efforts for a real parent partnership that works for each family. Why? Because it's good for the child.

OPTIMIZE YOUR KNOWLEDGE

1 What do you think when you read the statement **"The parent is the customer"?**

____

____

____

____

____

2 Describe the **"Why not?"** approach as if you were explaining it to a new employee during teacher orientation.

3 List the types of **surveys** you use in your program. What information did you discover from the parents' completed surveys that surprised you?

Certificate of Achievement

This certificate is presented to

____

for completing the professional development program:

Winning Ways for Early Childhood Professionals: Partnering with Families

__________ In-service hours

Redleaf Press®
www.redleafpress.org
800-423-8309

Gigi Schweikert
www.gigischweikert.com

The author and Redleaf Press have not verified the actual completion of the program by this participant.